NOT ONLY I

Chris McCully

NOT ONLY I

CARCANET

First published in 1996 by
Carcanet Press Limited
402-406 Corn Exchange Buildings
Manchester M4 3BY

A CIP catalogue record for this book
is available from the British Library
ISBN 1 85754 255 X

The publisher acknowledges financial assistance
from the Arts Council of England

Set in 10 pt Palatino by Bryan Williamson, Frome
Printed and bound in England by SRP Ltd, Exeter

Ed egli a me: 'L'angoscia de le genti
che son qua giù, nel viso mi dipigne
quella pietà che tu per tema senti.
Andiam, ché la via lunga ne sospigne.'
Così si mise e cosi mi fé intrare
nel primo cerchio che l'abisso cigne.

Dante Alighieri, *The Divine Comedy*, I: Inferno, Canto 4, 19-24

'And he to me, "The anguish of the people here
below paints my face with the pity that you take for
fear. Let us go, for the long way urges us." So he
entered, and had me enter, the first circle that girds
the abyss.'

trans. Charles S. Singleton (Princeton University Press, 1970)

For Ian Milnes and for Laura McManus
who guided me

Acknowledgements

Some of these poems have appeared in *PN Review, Summer Lines Anthology* (Manchester), and *The Observer*. I am grateful to the editors of these publications. I would also like to record my thanks to Cristina Nehring, Christa Nehring, Copland Smith, and Gavin Smith, who read and criticised extensive portions of the draft manuscript and suggested some necessary changes.

Contents

Song

All summer's unsafe,
the north wind and leaf,
its green turned like grief
on willow, white willow.

I walked through the places
I know that her face is,
found just empty spaces
and willow, white willow.

She told me the danger
I turned into anger,
and day made a stranger
of willow, white willow.

What loved me that morning
had failed by its evening;
what showed me the warning
was willow, white willow.

Now what I must mean
is north wind, leaf vein,
the summer worn down
to willow, white willow.

These eyes looking out
at what they must doubt
find no heat or light
but willow, white willow –

no heart's ease, dry blood,
ash turned in the wood,
green vanishing for good,
and willow, white willow.

Weathermap

Where has it been,
June rain, small rain?
What's the rain seen?

First it was river,
then it was weather,
cloud piled on sky
moving through May,

moving so slowly
not these eyes only
but birds and earth,
water and breath.

Where was it then,
small rain of June
on daylight moon?

Atlas and ocean,
fret of the sea,
and all their action
ending in you.

Chosen

Down all each day
to make you know
what could I say
to think of you?
And what could I
ask in reply,
except for choice
to hear your voice
come close?

Linger some hours:
those men in suits,
that second gin,
rich hand that puts
its balance in,
old face that frays
its leathers through
the lot it drew . . .
Unchosen these
fill up the ways
I could have bought
to walk your thought,
dear heart.

The corridors
of work and force
lengthen, what draws
my throat to curse
lasts far too long,
the words I wrought
go for a song
that was the sort
you doubt.

No doubt you blame.
I know you make
failure the frame
of what I take
from those I found

within your look,
my fault our name –
and yet it signed
what both forsook,
and recognised
what simplified
these hurts so they
were powerless
to hate, or worse,
to satisfy.

Today
mercuries climb
long afternoons
in heat; in time
whole honeymoons
bitter to taste
arrange their waste
unknown to those
whose panic chose
their marriage vow
and damaged brow
that will look back
on what was lack
of luck.

Compose the rote,
or otherwise
sustain the date,
the passing days:
ceremony chose
its strength for those
like us, who rate
each other's thought
but know too late
what cannot cure
the illness there
whose symptoms set
their cross before
our door.

What might have been
heart's light love turns
to all goodbyes.
Poet still burns
his pact in art,
endures his eyes,
ceremony and flame:
my fault, my blame,
our name and prize
go grateful to
the pasts they knew –
and let them go.
Letting you know
has made my choice –
your voice and face –
familiar pain,
whose talent takes
all my mistakes,
goodbyes and time,
and makes them rhyme
within this pen
again, again
makes art of loss
come close, come close.

Divisions

(for Sophie Hannah)

Those First Division sponsorships
amount to *Vogue* and reading trips
where everyone is paid and watches
the backs of fame on six large scotches.

The lower orders learn the game
is kick-about to fill a frame:
who's in, who's not, who's relegation,
who lives on last year's reputation.

Crushed by the heap, the bottom teams
are derelicts with hopeless dreams
where all the balls once went to Shilton
('O! safer hands than Adam's': Milton)

Some 'minor poets' – non-League sides –
get by on beers and maddened brides,
play foul for fun . . . Out of condition
we win our work through sheer attrition

and hit the bar for words that rhyme
no score or cup; no extra time.

The Inscriptions

What she left, not took away
touched me the more. Things can replace
with any cheque-book stub, delay
the shock of finding no known face.

Yet all that stayed involved our taste,
together's plural choices: how
undone and mine and run to waste –
the details hardly matter now.

And most, what had been given in
auspicious moments, smiling looks
whose wishes turned so peregrine:
all those inscriptions; all those books.

Imago

I made a woman out of what I thought
were odds and ends: this bit of hair that stayed
the night; that rag of hand; these eyes that caught
part clarity from sea; some wetted braid
pressed into service for the sex of lips;
and had it finished to the fingertips.

Thinking the making could delight me more
I gave the mouth a voice, a phrase or two
for pleasuring, and stuff I'd heard before
could satisfy a face to labour through.
(It wasn't easy: language is so much
the hardest part of knowing how to touch.)

Constructed; prime; aurally competent.
I called the name I wanted. It looked round
with something like surprise, or hadn't meant
including me in what its future found,
then spoke its strangled lexicon to fit
the silence half my lifetime made for it.

What I remembered, all I could afford,
the fragments that importance had to bind,
were nothing to her, simply kept her bored,
or whispered in the tissues of her mind
identities not chosen, not come true.
I'd disappointed her. She cost me you.

Bloodlines

September doesn't know what autumn's for
but killing windows, feathers in the house:
old blood marches away across the moor;
the connoisseurs of death walk up their grouse.

Lasting

I stay among the darkening staithes
where vivid evening slowly turns
to monochrome, and fret to wraiths
whose surfaces the river burns.

Sea-trout run shallows, run for where
there's nothing all that energy
must find but for the moor and air.
Their meaning was to last the sea.

And here I last the darkening
to lose myself wherever are
what sea and air move close, and bring
that past the night, that shooting star.

The Unaccused

I met my memory in the bar last night
impressing our imaginary friends:
those carrion countries, cronies his by right,
which woman's face put ruin in his glands,
the nights he'd spent mouth down, his day locked up,
his terms and comings, such a load of lip...

I'd given the same performance. Unaccused
I'd fed him all the lines and shames he used.
Their ashtray lengthened into years, his voice
betrayed his family tree another round
of double gins interpreting his choice
of hours and company as wished, as found...

He kept me in his unsteady blue eye
until last orders. Half his friends had gone
to silence or regret, not only I –
hearing his determined monotone
It's-closing-time-why-not-one-for-the-road? –
not only I, and yet I felt some pride

I'd said forever to the time his bride
had claimed forever hers. I must have lied.

His 'n' Hers

It's his 'n' hers today's big prize
stars show cash down is sure to prime
a bottom-drawerful of white lies
to dress to kill the fucking time

but not for them the future wrecks
the memories its money missed:
for her, moist fingers on her sex;
for him, no hassle in a fist.

Time Difference

Since you and I were spaced five hours apart
I checked your days against my watch all week,
your solitary breakfasts my first drink,
your evening book my last. And still my heart
beat half a night ahead, too fast to think
of anything but if things stayed the same:
if one was where the other couldn't look –
the Atlantic's separation of our name.

You moved within the life I'd left behind.
Elsewhere I talked, half blind, to any face,
wanting the earth to move the dark to wind
each hour-hand on our wrists to each right place.
In thirty thousand feet's returning blue
I saw sun rise at midnight. You came true.

Harm

While childhood watched the dry grass blazed,
marriages meant then tore their lace.
The harm let loose by that erased
whatever futures held her face.

The Facing Mirror

Not having children is the worst
redemption that my face is forced
    to choose:
whichever way I work the frame
    I lose

my looks in yesterday or blame
whose solace was a married name
    and days,
or wild assurance that this act
    would blaze

its mayhem down genetic fact
and make these features cataract
    on one
come flesh and solid by the force –
    a son

to share two solitudes, resource
through all the mirrors of Alas –
    and such
odd nothings that I've had to learn
    to touch.

(Look, now – my eyes shrinking to burn
the days they face so singly. Turn
    a hair,
and time will torch you out of care,
    my dear.)

It happens, happens, but not here,
no longer and not anywhere
    for this
amended mouth to instigate
    its kiss.

Too late
perhaps I talk too much; perhaps
the houses that I build collapse
            on air,
are vacancy and waste beyond
            this stare.

I slide from focus. Understand
my looking, you unfractured hand:
            it seems
I left dead ends and chromosomes
            for dreams.

Time Change

A butterfly in Peru has made the snow:
its wings beat once in sunshine, and the map
of pressure broke into a gradient bow
of isobars aimed from the Polar cap.

One quantum ripple gave tomorrow's range
its difference, suffered today's cold burn
through infinite amendment, casual change:
an insect flighting from a straightening fern.

And if that hadn't happened? Time would pass
into an altered spring, and you and I
would see the thaw reveal the yellow grass
in separate gardens catching separate sky
emerged from zero, accident and frost
whose purpose was to last the days we lost.

Bonfire

How to get rid of things is hard.
Another diary; starveling plant;
airport softback; Christmas card
whose tag then made him grin, now can't –

once made his life up, were his age
and all his eyes, and so deserve,
surely, some better harbourage
than flame. And he's not got the nerve:

to burn those old beginnings now
would waste the sum of their perhapses,
bring doctors to the smoke, allow
the marriage vows to show as lapses...

And so he won't. Somehow the space
will stretch, the books squeeze thin, the fire
be put to some more trivial use...
or so he tells himself, the liar.

The Autographs

Since she was cinema I'd be the dark
background edited to a flaring match,
an only point of light to stress the mark
all eyes must turn to just before they watch
come-uppance get her man, the night surprise
malpractice framed in furs, the gun still smoking...
  My purpose merely was to emphasise;
claim otherwise,
              she'll say You must be joking –

I struck him out of characters so lame
excuses couldn't bicker at the choice.
I was that star, myself, and learned to blame
the futures that depended on his voice
for gratitude and what could pass for pain
signing my name again
                  signing my name.

Genealogy

When years ago your family tree
assumed a distant line of me
the branch wouldn't endure the weight
and I became McCully, late
of Greenfield, home, and married state.

This wouldn't matter were it not
for eyes that watched while you forgot
reflections under the moon's horn
troubled by carrion and thorn:
my face, its children never born.

Walking the Village

More Yorkshire than they used to be, but drinking less
(and then only tap-water from the wastes of hills),
they reach the years of mortgage, pension, paying bills
with headaches happier than they'd thought at this address.

Although they've walked the nights all winter with the dog
(who misses nothing in his library of smells)
they're settled in the dark of hope for ne'er-do-wells,
have learned to wait for others' footsteps in the fog.

This is the community of the gone to seed
(treading the orange streetlamps back to house and life)
for whom it's hard – impossible – to face the wife
alone; that's twice as singly as we like or need.

Tea and Sympathy

(for Carson and Amanda Bergstrom)

All good advice talks down the shock
and glaze the leaver left for eyes.
I'm not ungrateful, taking stock
of in the red, the dark, the lies.

All's so unfair in love and war
good job the leaf invented tea.
I'd never realised before
how mugs were meant for sympathy.

Kingfishers

William Casson Long, 1923-1994

To look upstream to see that flash of flame
and cobalt blue made both our days, you knew;
knew how to give each river plant its name;
where nests were; how the current aimed, and drew
the fish in places all of us passed by –
but found you there, your second childhood on,
loving the seasons till the becks ran dry
and vanished underground to fault the sun.

Kingfishers come back; Langstrothdale is green
for April's sake; Grass-of-Parnassus grows
you showed me where; and what of springs I've seen
can't change the long perfection that you chose,
only augment the days it meant to last
on Watersmeet; the Stepping Stones; the past.

Wish

Too many years away
    to see
something I've done today
    will be
for someone's eyes alight,
    deny
the fact you chose, were right,
    meant me.

Landing

Late evenings through an open curtain
planes come down across the glass
to disappear beyond the hill
and houses parallel to mine.

Trust that the steel endures, set on
towards a night of altered watches;
trust that the landing lights align.
After all, you must be certain.

Dedication

Veering between
the delicate and the obscene
I slice the innards out
of rainbow trout.

My hands have tact,
deal well with bone, the head's impact
scored blunt along the blade.

For all the life I made
       this is my trade.

Scipio's Dream

He said he saw everything from a great height:
the water jug and cup, bulb in the bedside light.
He could hear even the smallest dust touching the floor.
It had all become impossibly, terribly clear.

Each afternoon he was wheeled to the window for air.
'What moves is angels, weight is love. The atmosphere
is flame, whose rings have stars for fire,' he wrote –
explaining himself away in his last known note.

The Headland

I know I took you to a headland full of bones
and called it holiday, but was it really just
for you to have nights' failure blame particular stones
and wish their future to fragility and dust?

Escaping you to fish, I concentrated through
the surface of the sea. It was like trying to pray,
but with no fixity to claim or trust in you –
and looking up again, seeing the horizon sway.

Denmark, 1992

Dust

Four things I trust –
the register of births, the power of name
and sacrament, finger with wedding band –
become the dust
that loves corrosion, brittleness and blame.
Corrosion I don't want to understand.
I must.

And so...But now...

Five aching limbs, a funeral next door,
divorce across the road, is middle age,
         my dear,
as is the wax on your too-cared-for car,
as is the slowness of your drafted page.

Don't say you saw it coming. Busy then,
you thought that years winced in another's eyes,
         the one
whose efforts hid his pension, meant Amen
but found your face, old essence of goodbyes.

And so they did. And so belong to you.
What hurts isn't the sum of what you've missed,
         but Now –
and sympathy, whose talents form a queue
oblivious to the fact that you exist.

Pillow Talk

This rig of head among a wreck of white
    not yours could be a trick of light
        to lift this hair and hand
           from shadow and
           possess the bone
      whose skin and face you own
   and will through all the years you mean
not mine although who knows they might have been.

Light

Snow at first light, what's left of darkness luminous
for winter's advocates, blind birds their trees and song.
Slowly the skylines come, not threat, no longer ominous.
I walk the ridge
    of January's air and edge
      with casual wariness
        whose worst I must have lasted made me strong.

The Shoe

There miles from anywhere you'd know
I beat the woods that latter end
of January for birds. The snow
had been a month, already thinned

to mud that clung to everything
and feathers, some collective head
(cocks only) that the dogs would bring
from ride and instinct, pattern, lead.

The drives wore on. Slower the breeze
collected wings and wounded, bound
the ivy tighter into trees,
became a frost become dead ground.

How far I went light wouldn't grow
the forest floor past peat; the dark
was absolute. Even the snow
held soft and black against wet bark.

And there, those miles from anywhere
and neighbourhood, in space that knew
few voices all its time and air,
I saw one single plastic shoe –

a woman's, white, and cheaply cracked
across the welt, where dirt and ice
had stiffened their contours into fact:
a woman's shoe. What sacrifice

or paradise had made it fit
whatever moment in God's name
and such a place invented it?
What second's guilt, raised hand, what blame

had hurt so much or been in drink
to leave a single shoe behind?
Or coitus came beyond the brink
of hurt to paralyse a mind

whose scheme of accident could put
a single shoe inside a wood?
Who limped away? Whose naked foot
was stalked? And whose mouth told the blood

what tall story to explain
its coming home to wash shame-faced?
What kind of Sorry came from rain
and pain or pleasure? Why the haste?

I looked around. Late afternoon.
The eyes of guns still trained on sight
elsewhere, on branches in the moon,
but it was finished, and the night

brought nothing more than walking back
the wood and that coincidence,
a woman's shoe. And yet its luck
or lack I've sometimes wondered since,

trying to forget that I was there,
those miles from anywhere. Pure chance,
of course, and chance that I should care
the shoe was hers, and evidence.

The Taxi

Whatever you think now don't let me know.
The taxi's waiting in your next affair;
it must be paid however far you go.

Someone will cash a cheque, prove hands that grow
familiar with your face as mine or air.
Whatever you think now don't let me know.

Hurt's habits need new clothes, a portmanteau
packed tight on tick and charged to anywhere.
It must be paid however far you go.

Load up the phones and memories. You owe
them nothing that suggests you came to care.
Whatever you think now don't let me know.

Doors slam on half a life that seems to show
goodbye can be as dear as it's unfair.
It must be paid however far you go.

Expensive exits, years of to and fro –
the meter running on your voice and stare:
whatever you think now, don't let me know
it must be paid however far you go.

Form

(for Steve Glosecki)

Not ready yet
    to sing a triolet
I practise hell
    to make a villanelle;
the crack of doom
    's the place for my pantoum,
which talks in code,
    says it was once an ode.

Ten whiskiesh glide
    into the line I elide,
and you can bet
    I can't rhyme two couplets;
my long ballad
    's acoustically mixed salad –
and what a ham I
    think I am to enjamb.

Nonmetrical (or
    'free') verse is quite a different
        thing,

of course.

Gold in the Hudson

Subtract the metal from the skin.
Don't mind that gold becomes the clay.
Walk down the wharf whose bridges burned
nine hundred wedding nights away.

Finger's lighter by a circle
whose years and diamond slipped their mark,
but flesh still wears its round of bruises
bent by pressure in the dark.

This river's full of marriages.
Don't stay to watch your wishing pitch
on oil and flotsam, floating lights:
enough to know the river's rich.

The Hammer

One went the hammer
    whose echo blow-flies fused on meat.
    Dogs barked at dust; as usual,
    mud fractured in the heat.

Two went the hammer.
    In its kingdom of age houses slept
    the mid-day out; as usual
    no promises were kept.

Three went the hammer.
    Wings scattered somewhere. Out of sight
    a name was cursed, as usual,
    and wouldn't last the night.

Four went the hammer.
    Hands fussed for water, formed on bread.
    Hours tasted wine; as usual,
    very little got said.

Five was the point
    as usual; as usual
        I nailed my Saviour to a tree
        for company.

Hiroshima

A thousand paper cranes define
new traffic   birdsong   people

that glitter of air and sound

and the shadow of a man
burnt into the ground

Japan, 1995

Against Seasickness

Climbing up the face
of the North Sea
I know the race is on
between drunkenness,
seasickness,
and me.
You think I take the grain
against the pain
my insides bleed.
　　　Indeed.
I say I need
this battery
of doctors, banks,
whisky, and therapy
to keep the industry
alive that tears
my stomach out.
　　　No doubt
if I don't drink too fast
the malt keeps pace
with all the worst
the North Sea's face
can summon – vast
corrugations built
from storm,
three hundred feet
of moving weight...
But take one drop too much
too soon and then
your shoulders heave and hunch
until you lose your lunch
at last, my dear.

Something you've eaten;
something I've grieved –
and both will reappear.
No winners here,
my clear-eyed angel. There
beyond the window

lashed to its wave
my world learns to behave,
if strangely
and in bits.

Dutch courage waits
with others' faces
that somehow fit
the bottom of this Scotch.
God knows my futures watch
their biter bit,
things have to change . . . But
I haven't even
got the guts
to say I'm sick of it.

Simply take...

200lbs. of shadow
and a worried man.
Cut into average pieces,
and sear over a naked flame
to seal in the juice.

Augment with middle age,
and season. Then

separately combine
a scant affair and overdraft
and set aside.

Add marriage to the meat,
with bouquet garni
of mortgages and pensions,
letters, photographs,
and wine to taste.

Allow to simmer,
checking from time to time
that the pan doesn't dry
(adding more wine and Epsom salts if so,
stirring continually).

Check seasoning, then fold in
divorce and impotence
(prepared earlier).

Remove from the pan,
and serve on a bed
of interesting courgettes,
decorating with some thinly-sliced guilt
at the last moment.

(NB. Not suitable for home freezing.
Do not re-heat.)

Reputations

Somewhere what lasts the book of names –
in ice and mill-dam, squall of geese
whose voice will go to Iceland by
some plummet in the compass and
another week of wave and air –
somehow this north ends up in flames

and lives on lips tasting of pride –
what's left of photographs, the box
in the attic, that grandson's jaw
some mirror caught for mother, or
so like so true the way he sat –
and burns the page that told it died.

Thinking

A kind of grief the fret of white that fronts a wave;
sadness also wet sand after the tide has gone:

the one a nonce and local, blind phenomenon,
the other, yes, a fixed and permanent condition.

Condensed Freud

So if he stood slope-shouldered, pulled a face,
lacked as a child all lineaments of grace
to front a lens, why should you be surprised
he got his sex in tissues bought man-sized?

Not Least

Hello the faces of my fair
since fair is left for company.
I take your illness everywhere:
it gives all memory dignity.

'Time is construction'

(Ilya Prigogine)

Time doesn't know itself as length or state
until a voice or hand can count it out:
between the lightning flash and thunder toll
the dark assembles into sequence all
those miles of moments merely as a proof
time is construction, distantly like love –

witness your face I left which came to last
beyond and mean the ocean I'd just crossed.

Cayuga Heights, New York State, 1995

A Sense of Balance

drinks the depressant last until
                    I'm free to make love work and home
it's time to take a midnight pill
                    and know some by-blow chromosome
stress follows slack I'm in control
                    to please society is bent
who gives a toss about the soul
                    to make the nightmare impotent
at least I'm chemically fit
                    to shut my eyes half-drunk half-numb
to feed and copulate and shit
                    keeping my equilibrium

On Greenfield Beach

The long drought North; the dark
become Polaris and
small constellations' reach
across the reservoir
dwindled to Greenfield beach
whose night and silence meant
the moment of your hand –

– my hand searching your face
for meaning made a mouth
open into a tongue,
come heat but not for speech.
Learning another grace
it found that all I knew
was lucky, there, and you.

Prufrock's Wallet

... But do I dare? Of course I don't.
The flesh that once was willing, won't:
a pack of three I bought to pitch
into some dunned pneumatic bitch
has shrunk inside my pocket book
and now's not worth a second look...

... A peach...
     and mermaids, each to each...
          a dildo and a pair of claws...

And memories immaculate
three rubbers past their sell-by date.

Another

It wasn't the fact
    of loving the one gone
        that made half night reflect
            his glass and blur, not then –

but when as could and would
    decided she took on
        another's ache and curd,
            and gathered them in.

The Exercise

The thing will have to be
re-done, but this time in
the language of goodbye,
full load, the weight of what
you are, no sympathy.

And no good looking clear
to all the end of effort.
That face now is nowhere,
and not to find, nor other
of its meanings coming nearer –

white cottage by the bay,
fires re-drawn each evening,
two glasses, a cloth, a tray,
the warmth of destination:
not to touch; never to say.

Pore over the map of pain,
the miles of ache and mistake.
You know the terrain,
the words you have to re-learn:
afresh; instead; again.

The Blazon

The pages burn my hands. I didn't know
what blazon was, what could be, until now –
can't quite believe your numbering means me,
or that the underscoring, message, cry
of happiness could fall onto the hard
resisting textures of a life still wired
to smiling desperation as its cause.
New voices break them open. They are yours:

but momentary; may not last; or come
to cat-calls in the dark on the way home.
Hurt, too, is real. Insult waits with drinks,
less charming than he seems despite his thanks.

And yet inside these sentences and way
of saying someone has been found, surprised
by the address, and accidentally
on purpose graced, and loved, and recognised.

Seeing Things

Tonight the lights came back, and gathered where
the dark would barely hold them as they moved
always just beyond a direct look
(a direct look would make them disappear)
and random as a wind-blown shower of sparks;
but left an afterglow even in closed eyes.

I didn't understand it then; don't now.
But if my seeing things means something clear –
a chanced-on frequency and love to show
how chaos to come burns on lit oxygen –
and if I think the showing makes a life
that's been and may intend to last, I know
the lights I saw tonight were all in all
the brilliants of my past, and were for you.

The Watch

If I've once thanked the moments as they passed
    for your embrace
the sequence runs to hundreds to the last
    that came across your face.

I do good gratitude, and know the count
    for what it cost.
The watch you left shows half the true amount
    and all the rest I lost.

Daybreak

a watch-face   merely
    part of the débris
the slow unwinding of uncertainty
    absorbed by night

come morning   surely
    time will not agree
there was fine wreckage   accidentally
    resume its right

to explain that only
    hurt convincingly
argues explosion's gift?
      Yes

          and for me
the rest was light

The Glass

A whisky eye
reads back its age
until the boy
it couldn't love
has formed the page
and language of
goodbye the boy
mistook for joy,
not only I.

The Apartment

Emptied of happiness it holds no air
but what was charged by every breath you took.
All the lights are down, and everywhere
such absence that I don't know how to look
to find your face in darkness, or declined
among what joy once was or might have meant.
Silence filled up the space before; behind
my going out, it is again for rent.

Something may wait – not certainty, not peace
except what counts as dustfall, but the strange
amendment of two fortunes taking place
surprise its emptiness, and come to change
a future void of vanity and goodbye:
obliteration's process; you and I.

Flight

Miles up I don't know where I am or care.
Pressure, fracture deliver me to air.

Without your hard completion nothing's whole.

I dreamed your body back across the Pole.

Ave atque vale

Who hasn't, sitting in isolation,
     come to the belief
they aren't worth half their object, passion,
     and are stiff with grief?

Lovers in unenviable apartments,
     knowing they're alone,
hug their unseduced deportments,
     eye the telephone.

Medallion-men on well-paid beaches
     are invariably sad,
keep for company three pet cockroaches
     and a client who's mad.

Drunks, slow on busy boulevards,
     could easily be us,
rambling for dollars in random words –
     love's point and terminus.

Hookers under lamplight crook
     a knee becomingly,
but however lucrative the trick
     the credit's temporary.

You're free. Everyone and no one bothers.
     I sing a face from air.
Each shares with poets and their mothers
     the culture of despair.

One always pays for conversation.
     Another's charged for joy.
Beloved's just a passing fashion
     whose pattern buried Troy.

Think on. Don't answer. To the knock
     where happiness occurs
consider what can kill the luck
     whose kiss and taste were hers.

I've learned not to reply. Although
I realise that pain
like worry tends to last, still I
won't say this much again.